Introduction

Imagine, you can live, work and run your business with less stress. You can live happier, form more harmonious relationships and take care of your health better. You can do it without 'needing' much at all.

It is a course of contemplation and reflection. It facilitates your transformation, a journey to your own inner peace, health and lifestyle of abundance. In a way, it is about setting up your own retreat – you will know yourself better and be able to focus on things that matter.

At the end of this course you would develop a system for your peace of mind and have tools at your disposal to use in your life to lessen your stress, combat busyness, eat better, be more emotionally stable and find meaning in your business or work.

This self-development course enables you to find your own point of enough where you feel at ease, content and with inner peace. This course is a program, a logical flow how you can adopt these tools for yourself and make a lasting change.

We have developed a unique MAKE framework that is fully described in our helpful course, so you can use it to create your own 'Enough Peace of Mind' Plan.

This course is not about minimalism. You do not need to bite the teeth just to sustain the diet or to control the anger. Values make these learnings easy to sustain.

At the end of Peace of Mind Course you will:

- Be kind to yourself by meditating and gaining more emotional stability, less reactivity to stress factors and profound inner peace. You will apply preventive nutrition concept to switch to a plant-based lifestyle without strain.

- Be kind to others by upholding a very simple but profound universal truth of non-harming others. Neither physically, emotionally or verbally. You will form better relationships and join communities you are happy to belong in.

- Find and re-connect to your intrinsic values. You will form your unique peace of mind system of people, things and activities that matter to you most.

This course will transform you from a state of 'never enough' to feeling satisfied, competent and complete with plenty of resources to enjoy your life right here and right now.

What can you expect at the end of this course:

- You will learn to listen to yourself and achieve lasting peace of mind in just 21 days or less. Our simple meditation instructions could be mastered by anyone and regular daily practice will enhance your emotional stability day by day. You're worth 20-30 minutes of your time!

- You will stop dieting but instead adopt a nutritional framework that will allow you to reach and maintain your ideal weight without calorie counting. All this is available in our free add-on to this course.

- You will learn about the so-called Point of Enough. This will help you to escape a rat race once and for all. Just in one short course.

Enough Is Enough!

We think we have been here before: we've told ourselves that 'I'm not good enough', 'my work is not good enough', 'my relationships are not good enough' or 'I don't have enough time for [your pick, but usually things that actually matter!].

At some point you just reach one vital realization: **enough is enough**.

We know what you want because we wanted the same – more peace of mind and joy in life, less stress and better health.

Sounds like a mission impossible, but it is not!

Mounting stress and increased busyness that seem like never ease on us are those characteristics of a modern rat race. Our lifestyle is programmed so we always want more. Businesses seem to be successful if they experience healthy growth. People are happy when their incomes increase all the time too.

What this does in a bigger picture for all of us is that we feel like we are not enough. Our business isn't good enough, our relationships might be not good enough and we are most definitely not enough as well. This feeling is like having a war inside of us. It is definitely not your much-needed peace of mind.

Busyness also means we don't have enough time. We might have money, but do we actually get happier with it, knowing that we don't live a very stressed out life. This constant lacking of something really hinders our inner peace.

We have been there.

You shouldn't single-handedly blame yourself for that.

First of all, it may only aggravate the situation. What's more, many things in our current world trigger these conditions, many systems are designed by clever people who want you to be busy, strapped for time and cash. After all, when you feel that way you are more likely to buy fast food or drugs, go to a loan shark or buy an expensive holiday just to treat or distract yourself. Big Food, Big Pharma, and many more Big corporations are very happy you feel that way. You are slowly but surely reaching your 'enough is enough' point.

    We invite you to learn how to rebel against these 'enough is enough' feelings.

CHAPTER 1

Current Situation

What's currently happening with us in our world?

Mounting busyness and stress, caused by our lifestyle that reminds more of a rat race are all enemies of our peace of mind.

On the contrary, they trigger the war within us – we start to feel that we are not enough (we lack something) or that we don't have enough money, or time or relationships. Our inner peace is hindered.

You shouldn't single-handedly blame yourself for that. For starters, it will only aggravate the situation. What's more, many things in our current world trigger these conditions, many systems are designed by 'clever' people who want you to be busy and strapped for time and cash. After all, when you feel that way you are more likely to buy fast food or drugs, go to a loan shark or buy an expensive holiday just to 'treat' or distract yourself. Big Food, Big Pharma, and many more Big corporations are very happy you feel that way.

Current situation is drastic...

- The food system is failing (1/8 of the population is in hunger and it is unsustainable to feed 9 billion people).

- Nutrition system is unhealthy with an enormous amount of sugar consumed, but also refined oils, processed carbohydrates and increased consumption of animal protein.

- Studies have also shown that increased amounts of blood glucose are associated with a rise of violent states in humans.

- Inequality is rising.

- 'Lack of time' and 'busyness' are all those words many people characterise their lives.

- General overconsumption and increased amounts of waste.

- We want more and more, and it eventually gets us in trouble.

- Stress is caused but a constant pressure to consume.

- Governments do not regulate sugar consumption, instead they prefer to regulate the weak; they do not regulate factory farms but instead, they prosecute animal welfare activists.

- Climate change issues and inefficient resource usage.

- Humans inflict a massive amount of suffering to farmed animals through confined animal feeding operation (CAFO) and focusing on quick and easy profits.

- Mental health problems are in the rise.

Experts agree that is these trends continue to grow, there is an increased risk of conflict, exploitation and poor health. Current generation might be the last one capable to reverse this damaging trend to human destruction.

Let's dig deeper into these 'systems' that make us suffer.

Many people get up early and then come back home late. Others work long night shifts that cause a wreck in their sleep cycles. This deliberate lack of time works for businesses who then offer fast food solutions or products to treat after a hard working day (sugary energy-dense foods). All these treats and fast foods are inherently low in nutrients, but packed with empty calories, trans fats and contain ultra-processed and refined ingredients. Businesses are interested in you keeping these very busy schedules and to only have time or energy to go and pick up those unhealthy takeaway foods. Industrially made foods cause various diseases, trigger obesity from a young age. Not a very happy picture for most of us.

There are more examples of such systems designed for people to stay in and benefit ultra-rich people – pharmaceutical and so-called healthcare (they would be happy to take our money to treat diseases caused by unhealthy nutrition), travel (holidays to treat us after a hardworking year) and so on.

Brazilian Fisherman Story

Let's illustrate one of the most common systems of employment and business growth with a fairly well-known tale about a Portuguese or Brazilian fisherman.

Imagine a small fisherman village. People go fishing every morning, later on, some of their produce is kept for them to eat and the rest is being sold at the town's market, so the villagers have enough money for clothing, other foodstuffs, occasionally medicine and home maintenance. They then gather together and eat, drink natural wine and dance. They share their life and ideas and enjoy.

One morning a fisherman encounters an American tourist. The latter asks him to tag along for his fishing job. Fisherman agrees. American tourist observes the fishing, how hard it is to just get a few kilograms of produce. He then starts to ask questions.

He asks the fisherman whether he could save money from the sales and buy a second boat. Fisherman nods.

American tourist then suggests that fisherman can employ his son to go fish with him but on the other boat so they catch is doubled or even more than that. Fisherman answers that it is possible.

American tourist enthusiastically continues and suggests that if it works out well, they could move forward with the same scheme and buy a few more boats, employ people and earn even more money.

Fisherman calmly nods and asks in return: 'What would happen then?'

American tourist, rather impatiently, answers that he could then retire in 20-25 years and simply spend enough time with his family, drink, be merry and enjoy life.

Fisherman agrees but adds 'I am already doing all of that'.

You see, it is easy to find yourself in that American tourist. It was also clear that the latter was programmed my society and systems that we need to grow our business all the time. But this rat race consumes you, it infects with greed. We are sick and imprisoned in this vicious cycle.

We join many systems as consumers. We start to belong to them and their creators. When you enter such system you are in a rat race – you want more, you need to spend more and you work more. Your life belongs to them now.

Rebellion

Therefore, the only way to liberate yourself is to create your system based on your intrinsic values.

We need to resist this power of Big Food, Big Pharma and other big businesses that make us sicker, poorer and stressed out. They do it at our expense too!

The issue of cost is that we do not pay the real cost. We hurt our bodies (the cost to healthcare), our wrong values hurt our communities (aggression, violence and crime) and these big businesses hurt our planet (polluting it and by killing billions of living sentient beings).

We vote with our money. What we do is that we simply let the Big Biz do what it pleases. We vote for our governments, but let them be lobbied by the Big Biz. We need to rebel to change this system.

This course is a quiet rebellion of every one of us. Quiet means we do it peacefully. Yet it also means we create our own 'peace of mind' system and live by it. We live happier, healthier, with values of kindness, peace and feel 'enough'. We are enough, we have enough and we can enjoy life.

Let's now go deeper in the course and find out what to expect from it. We then go on to develop our own goals and objectives for the course and beyond.

Part 1 Exercise: Your personality and current situation

Start by writing down what do you think are your main strengths and weaknesses. Let's call it your 'current situation'.

Most probably, some things troubling you. It could be stress at work or in business. Maybe some issues with your relationship. Or a feeling of constant lack of time or money.

Reflect all of these strengths, weaknesses and issues.

Try and note somewhere what would you like to change. A small notepad or an app like Notes would do just fine.

Before you dive in to move content of this transformational course, let's do more reflections and writing here.

Note a few things that are most important for you.

- What do you think 'meaning' is for you?
- Are you kind to yourself and others?
- What matters most in your life?
- Do you pay attention to people and things that matter most?

This is very important as you, together with our help with this course, will be taking yourself through the transformation to a point of lasting peace of mind. Many people call it happiness, but we suggest that inner peace and living with ease are just as great in our dynamic and always-changing world.

Let's get on with this course and we will show you how.

CHAPTER 2

Introducing MAKE Framework

"I'm not good enough,
my work is not good enough,

my relationships are not good enough,

I don't have enough free time,

I don't have enough money."

.. this list can continue …

Until you hit a realization: enough is enough

Let's allow ourselves a very bold but accurate assumption: we all want peace of mind, less stress and more joy, better health and more harmonious relationships.

We are all tired of chasing our 'never enough' feelings.

You are on a right path, as this Peace of Mind course will enable you to:

- Reclaim Your Feeling of Enough
- Feel The Spacious Inner Peace
- Treat Your Mind and Body Better
- Enjoy Your Life!

There are tools so you can:

- Start living with less stress
- Reverse many lifestyle-related diseases and get healthy
- Find plenty of inner peace and joy

Introducing MAKE Framework

It is of no surprise that **Meaning** is at the very beginning of our goal for lasting peace of mind. Many entrepreneurs will name you many M's that are important for a successful business namely marketing, management, money, mastery and so on. Though these are all quite secondary comparing to a meaning you assign to your business and life. Simply asking yourself 'Why?' gives you a boost of motivation, gets you to jump up from your bed and enjoy your day, even though it might be filled with challenges and obstacles. Meaning is not easy to define and it is not set in stone. Though living by your meaning will make your life happier and more fulfilled.

The other elements of MAKE framework work in synergy to help you to realise and live by your meaning.

Attention is the next element of MAKE framework and you won't argue that we do lack it these days. We lack attention to ourselves – how our body and mind feel. We also are constantly strapped for time to pay attention to people that matter the most – parents, loved ones and kids. We walk and do many things on auto-pilot without paying attention to things that matter too – a wonderfully bright sky or stormy tides in the ocean. It is of no surprise – we are bombarded by media, ads, texts and calls. It is hard to concentrate let alone sustain attention for longer. Yet attention to ourselves is a precursor to our physical and mental health. Attention to others is needed if we want to form harmonious relationships, be it at home or work. One of the main tools how we can develop attention is constant cultivation of our mind – listening to it, but also learning how to let go. Attention also helps to develop emotional stability and form a skilled approach to how to respond.

Quite naturally, with increased attention, you can develop and enjoy **Kindness**. When you are more kind to yourself, it is easier to make healthier choices when it comes to food and other lifestyle choices. No more strenuous diets, you are simply on a mission to treat your body with respect and kindness that it truly deserves. You are becoming more kind to your own needs. Attention to others helps you to understand that others have their issues too, but in a nutshell, everyone wants to be happy. Your kindness to others first spreads to people you love but then extends to others including all sentient beings. We all feel pain from now and then, but with kindness, we all can live happier. With kindness we value life and it becomes quite natural that we switch to a plant-based diet, care more about animals, interact with others employing care and respect for their life. Kindness allows us to accept things how they are and let go of something that doesn't matter to us that much. MAKE framework is truly about attentive kindness.

Finally, the meaning of it all, physical and mental health, intrinsic values and understanding of your needs make way to a feeling of **Enough**. The point of Enough is realised when our basic needs and wants correspond to what we have in present. It is not about living in a dream world or in the future. It is not about living in asceticism or with the bare minimum. It is about the careful assessment of what you want, followed by reaching the breakeven point (for yourself personally and in business) and then making one step further to arrive at a very comfortable point of Enough. This is where you are enough, you have enough – joy, health and happiness in your life. Point of Enough allows you to escape the rat race and live in the world of 'plenty'.

Stress is caused by the constant pressure to consume.

When you feel a constant lack of time it is similar to pouring oil on the fire. Point of

Enough allows you to transform from a state of 'sick and tired' to a feeling of 'plenty': enough good health, satisfying and harmonious relationships, contentment, joy and meaningful life.

You can see that MAKE framework consists of elements that work together in synergy. Feeling of enough is so difficult to sustain if you don't live by your meaning. Similarly, kindness is not working when you cannot pay and sustain attention to yourself and others. What is does though, it allows you to MAKE your own life. As you want it. Not as some 'systems' need you to be.

MAKE it happen!

Part 2 Exercise: Define Your Objectives

In order to achieve something, you need to identify your exact objectives.

You have already made some notes about your attributes and what matters most to you.

After you have just got an initial knowledge of our MAKE framework, could you assign your initial goals to the either meaning, attention, kindness or point of enough?

Reflect on your goals and design your objectives.

Go back and forth within this course and already start jotting down your own system of happy and healthy inner peace by writing down what's important for you and where do you think you need more work to be done.

Allocate some 'me' time and start reflecting and contemplating what's true to you.

Let's do some good work here!

CHAPTER 3

Building Blocks of MAKE Framework

Meaning
We start from an ultimate question – "Why?"

Knowing why you are in business, for example, may solve many problems, fill you up with enough motivation to persevere and move forward, and so much more.

Knowing personal 'why', or sometimes people call it purpose, does ultimately the same. We are very busy and trying to do hundreds of things a day with many of them happening at the same time. No wonder we may spend years before we even question why we do what we do.

We believe that meaning has a broader impact on everyone's life. To 'matter' is to bring meaning to the table of your life. Many of us want to matter.

One brilliant example of the importance of one's meaning was brought by a psychologist Viktor Frankl and his 'Man's Search for Meaning' book, which described his struggles in a nazi concentration camp during the Second World War. This book is timeless and remarkable, and meaning was indeed the main thing that kept Viktor alive in there.

Many business people are so concerned about money and marketing that they forget that should they lack the meaning to what they are doing, their work will be incredibly hard. We believe that many give up their businesses just because they lost (or never realised) the meaning of what they are doing. It can be incredibly hard to face so many challenges during just one day and the lack of meaning could be that breaking point.

So start asking yourself a question of 'Why you are doing what you are doing' (even if you are not yet in business). You reflect on what;'s important to you and many incredibly profound insights would be revealed to you.

Follow this course further to learn the tactics of how to do just that with our easy and straightforward exercises.

Attention

Have you noticed how our modern society values multitasking? It has been going on for years and many of us think that it is a skill worth developing. It cannot be far from the truth – multitasking is harmful to our brain and it results in attention deficit disorder.

On top of that, we constantly feel that we lack the time and when we finally get our few hours of 'me time', we may fixate on doing things that do not matter to us. This 'busyness' and constant pre-occupation negatively affect our ability to focus and sustain attention.

Following the prolonged multitasking activities, we are not able to work productively. It becomes more difficult to get things done, and what's more, we stop taking pleasure from what we are doing. Untrained attention becomes the cause of many modern diseases.

Here is how:

- We stop paying attention to our physical health, what we're eating and how we are consuming food. As a result, we are getting sicker.

- We are not attentive to our mental health and we let stress rule our world. As a result, our anxiety levels are rising.

- We do not pay attention to our relationships. As a result, partnerships break up and our world is as single as ever.

- We all could be more attentive to our inner values and meaning of our lives. We could live happier simply knowing we are creating a better life for all.

- Finally, we could pay attention to wider society and all sentient beings – our world needs better environmental protection and we should care much better for animal welfare.

The very concept of attention is about re-establishing and strengthening the connection. This connection leads to a greater regulation, which then allows creating a dynamic order. It is a signature of ease, of well-being and health. For this to take place, attention has to be nourished and maintained by intention.

Attention Deficit Disorder (ADD) is a serious dis-regulation in the process of attention. We can also see more often people developing attention deficit hyperactivity disorder (ADHD).

Learning how to train and refine our ability to pay and sustain attention is your so much needed U-turn back to what is most meaningful in our lives.

Let's hear from Alan Wallace PhD, who wrote a book called 'The Attention Revolution'. He said: 'Investigation into the nature of the mind is meditation and truly effective meditation is impossible without focused attention. The untrained mind oscillates between agitation and dullness, between restlessness and boredom. When we train attention, it has a profound impact on the character and ethical behaviour. Purification of the mind requires training in 3 things: ethics, attention and contemplative insight'.

So how do we train attention?

In the next part, we ask you to start noticing how do you talk to yourself. We learn about mindfulness meditation and how to meditate. There are plenty of scientific studies that show the benefits of meditation. We start small, but with disciplined practise, we can yield results in just 21 days of daily practice of just 20-30 minutes.

We are heading towards your profound inner peace and kindness to yourself.

Kindness

Once you start developing attention, you notice that you quite often talk negatively to yourself. Not surprisingly, people are unkind to their selves. It then goes further, so many of us start being unkind to others too.

The more you sit and reflect, meditate and learn more about yourself and things around you, the more open, receptive and accepting you become. It won't happen overnight, but with your regular practice, you'd start noticing these positive changes.

Similarly to attention, kindness can also be regarded as a skill. It means that you can train it and become kinder. It is not an innate quality that you are either born with or not. You can nurture kindness towards yourself and others.

In the next part, we introduce you to a loving-kindness practice. This is a meditation that will help you to deepen your thoughts and feelings of kindness and gratitude to everyone in your life including yourself, your friends and family, pets, acquaintances, but also difficult people and the entire world. It is a wonderfully warm and pleasant state of mind that you will develop.

During your meditation practice, you would encounter so many times when your mind goes somewhere. These places are sometimes pleasant but could be oftentimes negative or just neutral. Placing attention towards those thoughts and identifying them as such allows you to lessen the grip of troubling thoughts and de-stress. We are certain that feeling more at peace, less stressed out and more joyful, allows you to be more kind. When your mind is at peace, there is no need to hostility. You can nonviolently communicate with yourself and others, achieve your goals with kindness.

Hence our next exercise in the Tactics chapter is all about starting to label your thoughts. It is something that you can simply incorporate into your regular meditation routine.

Yet being kind to yourself and others don't just stop at what happens in your mind. Many people who are stressed out or simply mindless about what they eat or drink are being unkind to their bodies. Your physical health goes hand in hand with your mental health. That is why we've introduced a special add-on to this course which specifically targets nutrition. Call it preventive nutrition or one of kindness to yourself and others. Yet the main thing is that there are plenty of advances in the science of nutrition and by simply following our recommendations, you will transform your lifestyle for the better and healthier you.

In this additional mini-course on healthy nutrition, we discuss requirements, tips and restrictions. This is the way how many of us can prevent the so-called lifestyle diseases triggered by stress, busyness and very poor, mindless nutrition.

We provide scientifically proven guidelines for such transformation. You can use our internally developed framework, so you can easily remember how to make a healthy and nutritious meal, every time and every day.

Enough

A feeling of enough is a liberating force against rampant consumerism and our insatiable desires. What's more, it gives you the freedom to be as you are. You are enough. Sure thing, you have your strengths and weaknesses. Yet you already have everything you need to be happy.

Enough is an antidote for stress caused by the constant pressure to consume. Yet it is not just about material things. We usually forget that having enough time is our greatest asset

We realise that it is about enough of the present.

Be present is to be enough in the present:

- Enough for you
- Enough for people that matter
- Enough for things that matter

We all know a very popular saying: "There is no time like the present". Enoughness is a successful allocation of time to what matters most. If you can do it, you are enough, you have enough and you live a happy, meaningful life.

Our unique MAKE framework is complete with the identification of your Point of Enough. The previous reflective work that you put in makes it possible to re-connect with your intrinsic values to determine what's important for you and what you want and need from your life. This is your point of Enough. It is a point of your happiness and personal abundance.

This is where achieving peace of mind is different from minimalism.

We think that all our human progress should work for us and not against us. We discuss values of enough: your intrinsic values which ground you to be your best self. We discover how to find a point if enough both for you and for your business or work.

Values of enough logically give way to mindful consumption and meaningful and value-based occupation or business. It does not matter whether you are entrepreneurially inclined or simply want to have a better career, if you build it on the values of enough, you would be happier.

This is where you find lasting peace of mind.

Part 3 Exercise: Polish your goals

Now you know more about how MAKE framework can help you achieve your inner peace.

So let's go back to your goals. Allocate some more of so needed 'me' time, make yourself a beverage, get into a very relaxed state and let's get back to your goals.

To move forward and employ all the effective tools described in the next part, you need to further specify what matters to you, quantify your goals and make then as specific as you can.

Which ones do you think can be addressed with your mind, mindset and attitudes? Are they related to your freedoms (financial, occupational or mental), health or relationships?

List the goals and try making them very specific. It is probably a good time to think about starting a small journal

How important it is for you to achieve all those?

CHAPTER 4

MAKE Framework In Action

How to MAKE your life truly yours?

Peace of mind through cultivating your mind and living harmoniously with your true self. Accepting it. Being kind to yourself and others. Finding a personal Point of Enough for a feeling of sustainable inner peace.

Clearly, there are lots of issues. If it would be that simple, we'd be eliminating rat race, busyness, mounting stress very easily but it is all in our minds. Sometimes it is harder to work on it because as opposed to physical issues like your broken finger or something like that, the mind is not that tangible and visible. It takes a lot of skill to be able to look at it. Yet your mental health is equally if not more important than your physical health and wellbeing.

Let's go step by step and apply what we've learned already – practice makes it perfect and we've got some easy but very effective exercises to guide you through the tactics of our MAKE framework.

Please note that this is a much longer part of the course. Depending on your learning style and pace you may want to divide it into smaller chunks or, as an alternative, do an enclosed Preventive Nutrition mini-course separately from MAKE framework.

Connect with your tutor for more advice and guidance if needed (email).

Meaning: How do we find meaning?

We believe that Meaning comes first. It fuels your enthusiasm that spurs things into action. It makes it possible to persevere and not to give up when things go really bad. We all encounter challenges, big or small. Yet without clear meaning, it is just so easy to withdraw ourselves from these issues and to walk away. Entrepreneurs face these situations daily if not hourly. It is our utmost belief that meaning comes before money, marketing, management and other so-called M's.

Not surprisingly, as meaning is very important, it is also difficult to clarify. People are looking for their purpose or life's mission for years. Yet in our humble opinion, the meaning is more straightforward. It is an answer to a question of 'Why we do what we do'. If you know why you get up early or needed to stay in the office very late one day, it won't be a chore anymore. You will have the motivation and enough energy to see it through. It is not perseverance per se, it is a dedication to your meaning.

Ultimately, we encourage you to try and note some answers to the 'Why' question. Why your business is important to you? Why your career required sacrifice? Why you aim to spend more time with your family during weekends? And so on.

We invite you to try our exercise below but keep on working on identifying things that carry a lot of meaning for you when you learn to be more attentive, kind and enough.

Exercise 4.1: Last few years of your life

It may sound quite gruesome, but it is a very powerful tool. Sit in a quiet space and allocate 15-20 minutes for it. Take some notes when required. Imagine something has happened and you got to know you are left only a few more years to live. What would you like to do during these years?

Think about things to accomplish, things that are important to you. Alongside with your answers try to reflect on why those things are important. Why you feel a strong inclination towards doing exactly those things during your last few years of life?

Take some notes.

When you finish, check your list and find out how many things you are currently doing (which are on-going for you already) and things that you haven't started but they mean a lot to you. Compare this to your list of goals that you've created earlier on in this course. Highlight meaningful goals.

Now, think about things you are doing a lot of, but they do not carry any meaning for you. You should do them less or eve radically eliminate from your life. Think about some of your goals that may not have any meaning for you. Do you want to achieve them just because somebody else thought it would be nice to have? Maybe society though you need to do X and you just keep it ingrained in your life program? These are the things that keep you from enjoying your life to the full. You stress out a lot because you need to do them. Yet without any meaning, they become those awful chores that ruin your peace of mind.

Attention: How do we become more attentive?

Without any further delay we recommend to do a sitting reflection, consider it as your exercise too.

Exercise 4.2: Sit & Reflect

Now, let's make a cup of tea or glass of water. Sit and reflect – how did you address yourself just now? What kind of self-talk appeared when we were discussing issues? Was there criticism and some harshness towards your self? For example, we may be critical of our weight or appearance, but it goes further and are ingrained into our personalities when we start doing it constantly. We may start feeling as 'not enough', our work may seem 'not enough' and it is a precursor to a rat race and increased busyness. Many people think that being overly critical to ourselves helps them to be more productive or focused. What it does instead is focusing them primarily on the future whilst jeopardising the present. Again, current busyness and a feel of a rat race.

What about focusing on now. What about giving ourself some slack and just enjoying yourself for who you are?

Exercise 4.3: Enjoy Being

You can call it meditation if you like the word.

Let's talk about kindness, acceptance and feeling at ease and joy. Wouldn't it be nice?

You might have guessed it – we are going to be learning about ourselves, being ourselves in the present.

Here we develop a very useful skill – we re-learn your natural 'Being' mode.

Many issues come from our default 'doing' mode – we live for the future and we do things for it. We could also live in the past. What we proactively do in that scenario is we avoid things and avoid the present.

'Being' mode means you just 'be'. Yourself. Now.

Amazing things happen when you just be – your default mode lessens its grip and you live just here and now. 'Being' is characterised by a feeling of sheer awareness, being in the present. Some athletes say about it as 'being in the zone'. It doesn't mean you need to be idle in order 'to be'. You can be doing a lot of things – walking, talking to your loved one or walking wit your dog and simply just be.

We recommend to gradually develop this skill of 'being'. The first step is to experience 'being' whilst simply focusing on your breath.

Cultivation of mind or meditation is simply sitting and breathing. We will just build upon your previous reflection exercise.

Let's find a comfortable place to sit, allocate 15 minutes and just focus on inhaling and exhaling. Sounds very straightforward and also easy?

Well, this is what people call meditation. Mindfulness meditation is when you are aware. With time you can extend this skill to other activities.

Why sitting and breathing are good for a start? That's not just how it's much easier, but also it simply comes naturally.

You don't need to memorise a chant, anything else at all. You don't need to think about what to do, no need to engage with your 'doing' mode.

So without any delay – simply allocate 15 minutes. Sit and breathe.

If you want to ensure that your attention is on the breath, just count every exhale and inhale from 1 to 10 and then do start again.

Each time your attention goes somewhere and you forget to get back to 1, simply say 'oh, well' and get back to counting.

You 'learn' by making these 'mistakes'. Each time you remember or realise you need to go back to counting your breaths, your mind is getting stronger, more pliable, more capable to sustain the 'being' mode.

In essence, this is all about meditation you need to know. You don't need to think about it as something more than it is, like something divine or religious. There is something truly powerful in this simplicity – a vast array of benefits that meditation provides.

If you want to learn more, here is a link to a resource on countless benefits to meditation, collected from research papers by our friends at Ahimsa Meditation

Exercise 4.4: Create a routine

What you need next is to practice the above two exercises, namely Sit & Reflect and Enjoy Being regularly.

To do that, you need to decide on time and space. It is about routine that can be integrated into your life comfortably.

For your meditation practice to yield all these amazing benefits, and especially the ones that help you to achieve your goals, it needs to become a daily practice.

Choose the time, dedicate it for your daily meditation. Many like to meditate straight in the morning, when there are less distractions. Some like to do it after work or just before going to bed. The latter is especially helpful for those who want to get a better sleep. Meditation can relax your body and the constant rhythm of your breathing could be very calming.

Choose the place, make it quiet, and make sure you are not interrupted.

Now you know how to meditate. The main aim here is to try and make it a regular practice.

There are many helpful articles on our website if you are interested in learning more about meditation. Alternatively, for a very straightforward and secular practice, head to Ahimsa Meditation for some advice. We can also recommend a very concise and helpful e-book on Meditation practice how-tos which you can buy for less that $5 from our Shop online.

Start small. If you are one of those super fidgety people, start from just 5 minutes and gradually increase it to 10, 15, 20 and then 30 minutes.

The key is to repeat it daily. It doesn't need to be more than 30 minutes a day (no study has proven you need the quantity), but what counts is a constant practice.

So you daily 20-30 minutes of meditation practice with mean you would meditate for hundreds of hours within your first couple of years.

So now, start your routine and try not to miss your daily practice. You won't see immediate results, but researchers are convinced that even a week of daily meditation practice helps people to start re-wiring their brain towards a more peaceful, happy and healthy attitudes in life. Scientists are also convinced that 21 days of daily routine like that would help you to form a habit as you easily integrate meditation into your day. Enjoy!

Kindness: How do we start to be kinder?

We dive in straightaway into practice of kindness.

Exercise 4.5: Loving Kindness

Let's go even further and enhance your session with loving-kindness meditation practice.

You have been meditating for a while now. It is time to make a quick tweak to your regular meditation flow.

When you feel like finishing your practice, stay for a while and make sincere wishes towards yourself in this way: "May I be well. May I be happy. May I be safe and free from Harm. May I be peaceful". This is a foundation of loving-kindness directed to yourself.

It is now your turn to direct it to people you love the most. It would be fairly easy to do. Sometimes even easier than to ourselves. Continue and extend these wishes to your outer circles – colleagues, classmates, people you know briefly. It would be a bit more difficult but let's be generous – let's wish them all these good things. Next step will be alien to you at first, but please do try – extend these wishes to people you do not like, people who might have wronged you. It would be difficult and you may experience a set of frustrating emotions, but this is great – you know more and more about yourself. You gain a lot of peace of mind by doing so. Finish this by extending loving-kindness to all living creatures in this world – to oppressed people, to tortured farmed animals and just everyone.

Incorporate it and with some time you will see profound changes in your behaviour, relationships with your closest friends and family but strangers as well.

We also hope that you are now more comfortable with your own 'being' mode. It might be quite difficult in the beginning. We are living in an overstimulated with media and messages world, so being just you can be a bit weird. After all, you just sit and observe your thoughts.

Exercise 4.6: Label Your Thoughts

This exercise dramatically develops your kindness.

You can just be and let those thoughts be as well. They are what they are. They are not you!

You can look at them from the third person – simply label them for what they are.

First, you just name what kind of thought appears. For example, it may be something like 'oh I feel anger', or 'I worry about my work meeting later today'.

How do you feel when you have labelled (named) these thoughts?

With a bit of time, when you are comfortable to labelling your thoughts, make an experiment and remove 'I' from your labels. So it would be something like 'oh, there is anger', or 'here are some thoughts about the next work meeting'.

How do you feel now? Take some notes if you want to.

Do you think the intensity of the thoughts has changed?

We bet your answer is yes. The grip of those thoughts over you became a bit less. You are no longer so absorbed into them. They are what they are.

So if you have had an occasional bad thought, it does not mean you are a bad person. No way!

It simply means that there was a bad thought.

Yet what counts is what you do with it.

If you just act or react on that, it most probably won't be your most sensible option. But if you can take a pause (label it is from a third person), reflect (that it is not you, it is just a thought), and then say 'well, it came but it is gone now. So you do not act on your unkind thoughts.

This is how you don't allow unkind actions or even people in your life, to be affected by urges to react in-kind, rather than take a pause and realise that those are just thoughts. You choose to respond with kindness or let it pass.

This ability to respond to even most difficult situation without an aggressive and harmful action is one of the most skillful ways to leave with your peace of mind. Harmlessness brings inner peace.

Let's contemplate on this – killing is all around us, and we can feel a lot of anger or have some violent thoughts. But when we distance ourselves from 'it is me, I am violent', but rather 'there was a violent thought', you can respond to it. You will act according to your values. You have may intrinsic values but everyone has an ultimate one to treasure life and not harm others.

This harmlessness should be first of all directed at yourself.

With this easy exercise of labelling your thoughts and creating a distance between you and then you will stop your constant rumination, lessen your anxiety and worries.

You see now that kindness is not just an inner quality, it is skill because you can use mindfulness to extend your feelings of kindness to yourself, others around you, your closest circles first and then gradually to other beings on this planet.

Bonus: Preventive Nutrition mini-course

Preventive nutrition is key for your overall wellbeing.

We believe in saying 'let food be your medicine' rather than 'you are what you eat'. It is about nourishing your body and mind.

For example, many studies indicated that sugar can be one of the major causes of violent behaviour. Research also has determined that poor nutrition early in life predisposes people to antisocial and criminal behaviours and lowers intelligence. Bad nutrition regimen affects one's peace of mind.

It does work another way around too – if you are stressed out, with too many things on your mind and equally heavy workload, it is so difficult to think about healthy food. You have read about systems that make us suffer. Well, fast food companies that use trans fats, an excessive amount of sugars, processed and refined ingredients are benefiting from it. Similarly to pharmaceutical companies, they are completely fine with many people's poor eating patterns as they expect them to get sick and require medication.

Poor nutrition results in lifestyle diseases, lack of vitamins and minerals, bad immunity, foods that are injected with antibiotics, foods that simply make us sick.

If you look even bigger than your health, this picture becomes even grimmer – our current food system creates a massive negative impact on our environment, inefficiently uses our planet's resources, our healthcare system fails, we see a rapid rise in obesity whilst there are still hundreds of millions who live in hunger.

Yet there are some simple guidelines, that determine how to eat for your health, not against it. You can stop dieting altogether and manage your weight with ease. Our nutrition framework allows you to create your system of nutrition. You won't need super expensive or complicated meal plans. Everything is so simple when you apply your common sense and use only factual evidence about foods that make you healthier and avoid foods that can make you sick.

About our preventive nutrition approach.

We independently study and review science around nutrition. We have analysed the data and come up with a list of simple recommendations, the ones that make sense. It is the basis of our nutrition framework. You then decide what's important to you, what are your goals. You can adapt our framework to work for you and thus create your system. We have provided you with a sample meal plan so you could see how easy it is to go all-in and adopt a plant-based lifestyle. You can look for recipes and shopping lists to get even more help. Please share and communicate with other students [FB], but also get help when you are confused or have a question. Your tutor can help you too. [email]

We encourage you to get your first 21 days on the way and get closer to a healthier and also happier you. Be content in life with our preventive nutrition guidelines and framework.

The main theme of this plant-based nutritional approach is to avoid processed, refined and industrially modified products, especially sugar.

What? Meat and Dairy Free?

Meat and dairy are two hugely powerful industries that have created food systems that are making them rich at our expense. These businesses dominate supermarket shelves and many people's shopping lists too.

Most of us are so accustomed to meat and dairy that we think they are essential to humans and that we cannot live without these foodstuffs.

It is not true. It might have been the case many years ago, but not anymore. We do accept the fact – humans who lived hundreds of years before us did experience food uncertainty. It wasn't so certain as nowadays whether they could get food tomorrow if the crop is lost due to the weather or pests. Therefore, people domesticated animals and meat became a part of a diet. It was never a major part of people's daily meals and for many years only very rich people could afford it. Yet let's imagine your regular plate of food these days – you picture a big slab of meat and then maybe some veg or grain that you call 'garnish'. No wonder meat and dairy industries are very powerful.

Big processing slaughterhouses in the US process tens of thousands of pigs every day. Can you imagine how many lives we take just to enjoy a piece of bacon? These industries also employ top-class experts in marketing and advertising – they shift a focus from killing to making it sound neutral. They show laughing cows or pigs on a serene grass. For every one of us the product is called 'beef', yet what it is really – it is cow's flesh.

You will not find any reputable health study that will recommend eating meat or dairy. We have collected and analysed hundreds of scientific studies and discarded all recommendations that contradict each other, as a result we have identified a set of facts that are not only make so much sense, but they are also so simple to adopt. These recommendations will guarantee your best health, great levels of energy, prevent a myriad of lifestyle diseases and also, on a wider scale, save billions of sentient lives and protect our environment too. Let's dive in!

Healthy nutrition recommendations based on science:

- Consume only essential fats. Use coconut oil for cooking (mostly saturated fat but with healthier medium-chain fatty acids that metabolise into energy) and extra virgin olive oil (unrefined monounsaturated fat) for salad dressings and dips.

- Strictly avoid polyunsaturated fats and trans fats.

- Eat 1 tbsp seeds a day for a natural source of fats and omega-3 fatty acids. Good examples are flax seeds and also walnuts.

- Strictly avoid refined sugar and artificial sweeteners. Your sweet tooth can be satisfied by fruit and, if required, by less refined sugars. Watch out for high fructose corn syrup and other industrial sugars and strictly avoid it.

- Strictly avoid products made using refined white flour. Unfortunately, it will mean to avoid most of the supermarket cakes, cookies and confectionery.

- Plant-based whole foods provide enough protein for your balanced nutrition. Animal protein is not only unhealthy but also wasteful and immoral; it is completely avoided on a nonviolence nutrition plan. Industrial livestock farms are generating an enormous amount of pollution for every one of us on this planet and are the major source of the suffering of billions of innocent animals. Please say no to slaughter.

- Consume a healthy amount of complex carbohydrates. You should aim for slow sugar releasing ones with lower GI/GL and higher in fibre. You can get enough fibre from whole grains, oats, pseudo-grains like buckwheat and quinoa.

- Avoid dairy. You will get healthy protein and enough calcium from plants. Factory farms with inhumane violent attitude to animals should be boycotted.

- Do not obsess with calorie counting but be aware of your calorie requirements. Sedentary or active lifestyles and different age groups will all require adjustments.

- After collecting all these recommendations that do correspond with common sense so much, we could devise a simple nutrition framework.

Peace of Mind plant-based nutrition framework:

Fat: 1 tbsp ground seeds or cold-pressed seed oil

Protein: 3 servings of beans, lentils, quinoa, tofu or seitan

Complex carbs: 4 servings of whole grains: brown rice, millet, rye, oats, corn, quinoa, whole wheat bread or pasta.

Fruits and vegetables: 6 servings of various fruit and veg, try to always have dark green leafy vegetables on your plate.

Additionally, drink at least 6 glasses of water, herbal or fruit teas. For great gut health always eat enough fibre, approximately 35 grams a day for sure. Great sources are beans, lentils, oats, broccoli, avocados, apples, carrots, beets, chickpeas, almonds, chia seeds, sweet potatoes and even chocolate. A great tip to assess how 'whole' is your food: check the nutritional contents and if the amount of fibre is less than the number of carbs divided by 6, it means that your food is processed (some are astonishingly low in fibre and should be avoided).

You need to avoid burnt and heavily browned food.

Avoid preservatives and chemical additives. Minimise your alcohol, tea and coffee intake to 2-3 drinks a day.

Lifestyle choices should also include enough exercise – think about at least 10000 steps a day, some morning stretching or yoga, but also cardio and weight exercises for an hour 5 times a week. Surely, you can find 5 hours a week for your health!

You can see that these recommendations and framework exclude meat, eggs and dairy making this framework ultimately vegan. It wasn't our goal, but the only scientific evidence that clearly showed what is truly good for your body indicated that meat, animal-derived fats, eggs and dairy are harmful.

Eating plant-based contributes to your inner peace and well-being.

Ancient philosophers and scientists like Hippocrates and Epicurus, but also other prominent figures like Darwin, agreed that inner peace benefits digestion, so there is a joint link between our mind, emotions, nutrition and well-being.

Albert Einstein agreed with them saying that "Nothing will benefit human health and increase the chances of survival of life on earth as much as the evolution to a vegetarian diet".

Dr Michael Greger, in his book "How not to die" added that "we eat as if the future doesn't matter". He connected our nutritional choices not just to our health but also to the state of our environment. Animal flesh is not only wasteful environmentally, but also morally and even more so to our own body.

Some people think about vegetarian diets as either too limiting or refer to them as utopias. It is neither as it is all in our hands. People agreed with this since the times of Pythagoras, who said "As long as men massacre animals, they will kill each other. Indeed, he who sows the seeds of murder and pain cannot reap joy and love". He was spot on how interconnected it all it. Our actions have direct consequences to our health, physical, mental and emotional.

Further on, Henry David Thoreau said: "I do not doubt that it is a part of the destiny of the human race, in its gradual improvement, to leave off eating animals, as surely as savage tribes have left off eating each other when they come in contact with the more civilised".

Implementation

If you will incorporate the above suggestions, it is clear that the approximate split between macronutrients namely carbohydrates, fat and protein should be 75/15/10.

Please do not be alarmed by high carbohydrate contents, it is recommended to cut all refined and processed types of them and replace with whole foods like beans, legumes and vegetables. The latter will also give enough natural sugars.

Whilst there is still a debate on fat consumption, there is no argument that there are some essential fatty acids that help us to absorb fat-soluble vitamins, it is as simple as this. Therefore the above requirement to cut all trans fats and polyunsaturated fats (like canola and other heavily processed oils) and replace them with moderate amounts of extra virgin olive oil for dressings and coconut oil for sautéing and stir-frying.

Some of you might be also surprised of such a low recommendation for protein intake, yet consuming only high quality plant-based whole foods will provide all required amounts of protein you need, make sure it is around 0.7 – 0.8 g per kg of your weight. My figure of 64 grams is very easy knowing that I love hummus (chickpeas), tofu and other pseudo-grains like quinoa and buckwheat. Red kidney beans are not just very rich in iron but contain up to 30% of protein per weight. The only exception to this would be for teens and very elderly, there is some evidence, that this requirement should be increased slightly to enable a better repair and growth for them.

This plant-based nutrition approach helps to achieve better health by means of being kind to yourself and others, which means no killing, treating your own body better, cooking for your loved ones, sharing and enjoying a meal together.

Start with planning your week. Prepare what you can in advance. Put in containers and refrigerate what needs to be. Get staples like beans, rice, quinoa, and more for your cupboard. Buy seasonal vegetables in your local store and create delicious meals that take less than half an hour for sure.

Learn from what worked well. Link your improved nutrition to your lasting peace of mind.

Exercise 4.7: Recipes wish-list

List the dishes that fit into the framework that you would like to eat. Search the Internet for recipes and categorise them into breakfast, lunch and dinner. Spend just 20 minutes and you will get at least 20 delicious plant-based recipes for each category. Choose only the most delicious ones that you can't wait to try!

This is the end of the Preventive Nutrition mini-course. We hope you found it useful and will come back to these recommendations and the framework in order to implement it step by step.

Kindness continued

We continue with Kindness for now and it may come to you as a surprise that many struggle with learning how to be kind to their own selves. Acceptance brings us closer to feeling at peace inside.

Exercise 4.8: Ultimate Acceptance Skill

Ultimate acceptance is a mindset that grounds you and helps you be at peace with yourself.

When looking outwards, acceptance also lowers your stress levels. It happens because accepting the situation, it helps to lose the negative grip over you. You can come back to a state when you are kind to yourself.

Harmlessness to yourself is key, you will feel peace, you can respond better to stress, to others around you. Accepting yourself as you are is, therefore, becoming a very key skill to feel at ease with yourself.

So we can see that harmlessness to ourselves bring an enormous inner peace and peace of mind.

Yet you do not live in isolation, so your peace of mind is only possible when you can extend this kindness to others.

Using all the earlier exercises helps to build on understanding yourself better, treat yourself with kindness and extend it to others. Therefore this exercise is simply about sitting down and reflecting on accepting yourself and others as they are.

Please allocate some 'me time', be it just 15-20 minutes and reflect on accepting yourself as you are, but similarly, accept others as they are. The world is just the way it is.

Enough: What do we do to live with a profound sense of enough?

As we discussed previously, finding your point of Enough is really important for your lasting peace of mind. All previous components of our MAKE framework serve the same purpose, they help to identify your needs and wants, become attentive to what's important to you, what matters most and then be kind to yourself and others during your life journey.

To identify your Point of Enough, we will need to ask you to do the following exercise. You will certainly need to do some notes and even calculate a bit. Nothing strenuous.

Exercise 4.9: Find Your Point of Enough.

Let's start with something that is called a breakeven point. Begin with yourself and calculate your expenses (only required ones). This figure indicates how much of income you need to earn to simply afford your basic needs.

If you run your business and do not know this future on top of your head, do the same with your business too. You need to know where is that breakeven point.

Next step is to go further and incorporate expenses that you will want to spend as they carry a lot of meaning to you. For example, investing a quarter of your income to a new business venture or saving money for family holiday twice a year. In terms of business, it could be hiring another employee so you have some room during the day to spend on strategic things.

Get all your previous notes, how much money all those meaningful goals require? How much money is needed so you and your family eat healthily? You can add all your most meaningful things that you identified earlier.

The idea is that you will come up with an extra budget that you need to feel happy and fulfilled. As though your last years are gone and you'd feel like you've done those things that are most meaningful to you. As a result, you are now coming up with a figure of how much you need to earn to be able to do all that.

Most people are surprised when they do the math that it is not much. Your point of enough is most certainly bigger than the breakeven, but when you think about the figure it is usually very achievable.

We have seen so many people saying that they already have enough. As you've seen earlier on, we may bug ourselves with these constant 'I am not enough', or 'I don't have enough money' feelings simply because we are trapped in a loop that is created by systems and marketers. Systems want you to consume, as mindlessly as possible. When you do that, it is not enough, it is about 'never enough'.

This approach is very simple, but it invites you to consume mindfully and live with the sense that you are enough as a person (sure you are, you live by your values and do the things that are meaningful to you) and you have enough (you know your point of enough and you are either already there or on the way).

CHAPTER 5

Plan To MAKE Your Life Truly Yours

MAKE a plan!

This is your actionable part of the course where you can put the above knowledge into practice that will work specifically for you.

You have identified your objectives based on the issues that matter most to you. You are familiar now with MAKE framework that helps you to address the issues and achieve your goals. You have been equipped with a vast array of knowledge and tools how you can add meaning, attention, kindness and values of enough into your life.

It is time to MAKE an actual plan.

Please get your previous notes when you have explored your personal strengths and points of improvement. Here we encourage you to use your reflections that you've accumulated during this course. It enables you to MAKE this action plan truly yours.

Part 5 Exercise: MAKE a plan

Create a table using these instructions:

- Start with creating a column answering a very important question 'What do I want?' (List all your goals you've identified earlier on, be it connected with your health, business, money, relationships and so on).

- For each of your objectives write 'What do I have to do to reach it?' (For example, when thinking about improving your health, your possible ideas may contain switching to plant-based, eliminating sugar and stop eating so much white bread)

- Again, for each of your goals and actions, add a note about 'any support and resources that I need' (Following our previous example, you may want to seek good plant-based recipes online, attend a cooking class, allocate more time to cook from scratch and so on)

- Each goal now needs to include its 'Success criteria' (How would you know you did it? For example, it could be something like 5 pounds lost in the next month)

- Finish by specifying a 'Target date' when you will review (As we said, next month is going to be a good start to check on your weight)

You are now in the process of designing a system of your peace of mind.

This table of your MAKE action plan is based on your goals. Start on implementing all the action items. See what has worked well, what has not.

You are not alone with it. You can discuss your experience, findings and learnings with our community on Facebook (here is a link to our page) or tutor (simple send them your email)

Maximize on your progress by setting realistic plans on where, when and how

You are now proactively bringing peace of mind and inner peace to your life. Let's finish the course by giving you an extra helping hand to go with the flow of these changes smoothly.

CHAPTER 6

MAKE It Happen

MAKE it happen for you

Ultimately, during first few days or weeks of anything new that came to your life as a habit or a small action item, you want to monitor how is it going and be mindful about it. It's sometimes way easier to deal with setback or even just doubts by getting help from others by accessing our dedicated Facebook page and tutor email. Engage!

Facing obstacles

First of all, in order be ready to get going and be disciplined with your meditation practice or find time to cook plant-based food from scratch or even contemplate your meaning in business, try to answer the question "Why?". This simple question will get you up earlier in the morning to do your meditation.

Sometimes your usual busy schedule will be a huge obstacle. What we see with many of our students is that if you create your system of peace of mind, this busyness lessens and you will find time to do things that most important to you with ease. Right now you are still in a rat race and give yourself some slack because of that. You are on the way to make the system work for you, not against you.

Common Sense Rules

You will hear the opinions of others. First of all, you do not need to explain anything. You are doing this course for yourself. It may sound selfish, but you can't change the world or even your immediate social circles without changing yourself and living how you want to live.

Be selfish, allocate some time for your practice, or cooking, or meaningful business and be happy about it.

If others criticize, don't pay attention to that. If you feel like joining a debate about peace of mind, do so too. Many people are non-believers that one can live their life with much less stress, busyness, strive on foods that are made without harming living creatures and enjoy their meaningful work.

Finally, if you feel like you can turn objections into support, recommend them to try this course. We offer a discount for your referrals and you would also earn some rewards for yourself.

Get Help

Right after you are done with creating your peace of mind system, we also provide you with tons of tips and tools for you to implement the changes with ease.

We cannot think about all the possible situations, so it would be great if you share your progress or thoughts with other people who are doing this course. For this, we've created a [Facebook page](#) for all the learners like you.

Finally, we have a team of coaches, who are busy providing their expert help to students and other clients. Your course includes several hours of our experienced tutor support – you can ping them over [email](#) or whatever way is more suitable for both of you.

Recommend Peace Of Mind School

Sponsor a friend to help them MAKE their life, buy them this book or send them online to [peaceofmindschool.com](#).

CHAPTER 7

A Short Afterword

Many Thanks

We at Peace of Mind School truly hope the course changes hundreds, thousands, if not millions of lives for the better.

Our very dynamic and sometimes crazy world doesn't allow us to freely stop, pause, reflect and live more mindfully. Hence many issues that we encounter on a daily basis in our lives, societies and the whole world.

Yet you can MAKE your life truly yours. Living more mindfully, with health and kindness, with harmonious relationships and with the business that brings so much satisfaction and joy – you are able to achieve all this.

Empower your business, entrepreneurial spirit, body and mind.

There is not better time like the present. MAKE it happen now.

Copyright PeaceOfMindSchool.com, 2019-2020

© *All Rights Reserved*

No part of this publication may be reproduced or transmitted in any form by any means without prior written permission of the copyright owner of this book and course.

ISBN: 9798637782321

www.ingramcontent.com/pod-product-compliance
Lightning Source LLC
Chambersburg PA
CBHW070300220526
45465CB00004B/1683